Contents

Berries for Life. A natural way to stay younger.

Berries for Life

A natural way to stay younger.

Dr. Joyce Tellier Johnson BSc., ND

ISBN 978-0-9782797-0-7

Printed in Canada.

Introduction

Berries — a simple subject, right?

They are tasty, juicy little bundles of natural goodness that have some real, proven health benefits. But once the scientific and medical experts start talking about "anthocyanins, polyphenolic compounds and phytochemicals" do you get a bit fuzzy on the subject of berries?

Whether you pick berries "au naturale", berry juices, concentrated extracts in capsules or combination supplements containing the "best of the berries", you can turn to these pages for easy to understand definitions and an explanation of how berries can help you enjoy better health, for life.

Pick your favorite berry

Which berry do you like best? Strawberries? Blueberries? Raspberries? Cranberries?

No matter which you "pick", berries are well-loved for their flavour and the fact that many of them can be eaten straight from the bush. However most of our favorite berries have relatively short growing seasons so getting plenty of them in a fresh state is not always easy. Once you learn just how much these colourful fruits support and enhance health, you will want to fill your freezer and investigate other ways to "pick" berries all year long.

In these pages Dr. Joyce Tellier Johnson gives you many ways to get the best of berries for the very best health enhancement.

the Editors

Berries for Life. A natural way to stay younger.

The Language of Berries and Health

When you talk about the benefits of berries, or any natural substance, you are crossing over into the realms of chemistry, bio (life) chemistry and medicine. The terminology can seem quite overwhelming — not unlike the techno-jargon used to discuss computers — however most terms are combinations of simple root words from Greek or Latin and once you know them, you can understand whole categories of scientific terms. Understanding the terminology related to these colourful fruits can help you make healthy choices, plus, you can sound like a real expert at your next social gathering!

Tackling the Terminology

Antioxidant — a nutrient-sourced molecule that can neutralize unstable free radical molecules and prevent them from damaging cells. All living cells contain complex systems of antioxidant chemicals and enzymes to prevent chemical damage to the cells' components by oxidation. A diet rich in phyto(plant)nutrients will provide thousands of different antioxidants to the body.

See page 9 for a detailed explanation of free radicals, oxidation and antioxidants.

Anthocyanins, Anthocyanidins & Proanthocyanidins

antho = flower in Greek
cyan = Greek for blue or purple (kyanos)

Anthocyanins are any one of a group of pigments (colouring agents) formed in the cells of plants which produce the deep red, blue, purple and lavender colours of petals, leaves, roots and fruits.

Proanthocyanidins may also be called OPCs for oligomeric procyanidins or PCOs for procyanidolic oligomers. These are a class of nutrients belonging to the bioflavonoid family. Proanthocyanidins have antioxidant activity and play a role in the stabilization of collagen and maintenance of elastin, two important proteins in the body's connective tissue. These compounds have been reported to reduce swelling after surgery, to strengthen capillaries, and to improve eye health and vision, as well as helping to prevent or reverse abnormal blood clotting in smokers.[1]

Proanthocyanidins can be found in pine bark, grape seed, grape skin, bilberry, cranberry, black currant, green tea, black tea, and other plants. Nutritional supplements containing proanthocyanidins from various plant sources are available, alone or in combination with other nutrients.

Berry — In botany, the study of plants, a berry is a fruit in which the plant's entire ovary wall ripens into an edible outside layer or skin. The seeds are embedded in the flesh of the ovary. According to this definition, the tomato is a berry and the strawberry is not. The fruit of citrus plants, such as oranges and lemons, are a modified form of berry called a *hesperidium*. In common language the term "berry" refers generically to any small, edible fruit with multiple seeds. Berry will be used throughout this booklet as the generic term for these fruits.

Bioflavonoids (see Flavonoids/Flavones)

Carotenoids — naturally occurring pigments, usually red, orange or yellow in color. They are found in many plants and foods and are used extensively as safe, natural colorants for food, feed, and cosmetics. They are essential for plant growth and photosynthesis, and are a main dietary source of vitamin A in humans. Carotenoids have been associated with reduced risk of several chronic health disorders including some forms of cancer, heart disease and vision degeneration.[2]

Chemistry/Biochemistry — the word chemistry is derived from the word "alchemy", and originally from an Arabic word that meant the art or science of melting and mixing metals. Alchemy included the first efforts of mankind to combine and alter substances. The storybook alchemist was usually a wizard-like character who wanted to turn lead into gold.

Chemistry deals with the characteristics of simple substances and the changes that take place when these are combined to form new or different substances. Biochemistry is the subject of the components of *living* things and how they combine or alter, usually at a cellular or molecular level.

Ellagic Acid — Used in alternative medicine to prevent cancer, ellagic acid can be obtained from strawberries, cranberries, walnuts, pecans, pomegranates and red raspberry seeds. Ellagic acid is pharmacologically active and has been found to control haemorrhage (severe blood loss) in animals and in humans.[3]

Fibre — Dietary fibre is the term for plant materials that your body can't digest. Fibre is classified as soluble or insoluble. Soluble fibre has been shown to help lower blood cholesterol. Oats have the highest proportion of soluble fibre of any grain. Other foods high in *soluble* fibre include beans, peas, rice bran, barley, citrus fruits, strawberries and apple pulp. Fibre, soluble or insoluble, is an important aid in normal bowel function. Foods high in *insoluble* fibre include most whole grains, cabbage, beets, carrots, Brussels sprouts, turnips, cauliflower and apple or berry skin.

Flavonoids/Flavones — classes of water-soluble plant pigments. Flavonoids occur in most plant species. Flavonoids have been shown to have antibacterial, anti-inflammatory, anti-allergic, antiviral and potent antioxidant activity, which may be the most important function of flavonoids.[4] A great number of plant medicines contain flavonoids. There are various classes of flavonoids: flavanols, flavanones, flavones, flavan-3-ols (catechins), anthocyanins, and isoflavones. Functions of flavonoids in plants include intensifying flower petal color, attracting pollinator insects, and acting as anti-microbial agents. Bioflavonoids is often used but "bio" simply means "biological in origin", hence all flavonoids are bioflavonoids.

Free radicals — are unstable molecules that "steal" electrons from other molecules, creating more free radicals and ultimately damaging cells and speeding aging and age-related conditions.
See page 9 for a full explanation of free radicals and antioxidants.

Gallic acid — Gallic acid is an organic molecule that seems to have anti-fungal and anti-viral properties. Gallic acid acts as an antioxidant and helps protect cells against oxidative damage. It has been shown to fight cancer cells, without harming healthy cells. Gallic acid is a component of blueberries and certain other berries. It is astringent and is recommended for diabetes management.

Helicobacter pylori — This is a bacteria that has been shown to be responsible for the formation and continuation of peptic ulcers. Cranberry juice and extracts may help prevent ulcers by making it difficult for the H. pylori bacteria to stick to the lining of the stomach. More research is being done.

Lignans — Lignans are chemical compounds found in plants. They are one of the two major classes of phytoestrogens, antioxidants found in certain plants including flax seeds, pumpkin seeds, sesame seeds, rye, soybeans, broccoli, beans, and cranberries. Lignans are being studied for possible use in cancer prevention, particularly breast cancer. Like other phytoestrogens (such as soy isoflavones), they hook onto the same spots on cells where estrogen would attach. If there is little estrogen in the body (after menopause, for example), lignans may act like weak estrogen; but when natural estrogen is abundant in the body, lignans may instead reduce estrogen's effects by displacing it from cells. This displacement of the hormone may help prevent cancers, such as breast cancer, that depend on estrogen to start and develop.[5] Lignans may have other health benefits as well. Further research is underway.

Nutraceutical — Any substance that may be considered a food or part of a food that provides health benefits, including the prevention or treatment of disease, can be called a nutraceutical. This includes isolated nutrients, whole foods and even genetically engineered "designer foods".

The term "nutraceutical" was coined by The Foundation for Innovation in Medicine in 1989 and has become part of the standard language of the medical, scientific and natural health communities, as well as the food and drug industries.

Oxidation, oxidants, oxidization — Oxygen is a vital element in all living cells. Oxidizing or oxidation refers to the combination of something with oxygen; burning is one kind of oxidation, rusting is another. At a molecular level oxidation means that electrons are lost from molecules due to chemical reactions. Oxidation can produce unstable molecules called *free radicals* (see page 5) that grab electrons from other molecules, destabilizing them.

See page 9 for the full story of oxidation and antioxidants in the body.

ORAC—stands for Oxygen Radical Absorbance Capacity. It is a test tube analysis that measures the total antioxidant power of foods and food components.

Phytochemicals—a general term for naturally occurring chemicals found in plants

Polyphenols/Phenolic—a group of antioxidant chemicals found in plants, including most legumes, apples, blackberries, cantaloupe, cherries, cranberries, grapes, pears, plums, raspberries, and strawberries; and in vegetables such as broccoli, cabbage, celery, onion and parsley.

Proanthocyanidins, PCOs or OPCs—is a class of flavonoids discovered in 1936 by Professor Jacques Masquelier and called Vitamin P, although this name did not achieve official status and is not commonly used. Masquelier developed techniques for extracting Proanthocyanidins from certain plant species. See Anthocyanins above.

Quercetin—a flavonoid that forms the "backbone" for many other flavonoids. Quercetin is found to be the most active of the flavonoids, and many medicinal plants owe much of their activity to their high quercetin content. It has demonstrated anti-inflammatory activity and it inhibits manufacture and release of histamine and other allergic/inflammatory mediators. Quercetin is also a potent antioxidant.[6]

Resveratrol—an antioxidant plant substance found in the skins of dark-colored grapes, and concentrated in red wine. Pterostilbene is a variation of resveratrol, abundant in *Vaccinium* berries (like blueberries and cranberries).

Salicylates/Salicylic Acid—Berries may also help prevent heart attacks because they contain a natural form of aspirin called salicylates. British researchers analyzed the blood of subjects who were not taking any form of aspirin or drugs containing salicylates. They found salicylic acid and two related compounds present in blood, presumably from dietary sources, including raspberries and blackberries. Researchers at the National Center for Health Statistics (NCHS) in Hyattsville, Maryland also established a connection between reduced risk of heart attack and increased intake of salicylates.[7]

The Shared Benefits of Berries

Antioxidants for Lifelong Health

One of the basic ways berries contribute to our health is through their antioxidant power. Antioxidants are natural substances found in plants, which help strengthen cells and thus prevent disease, boost immunity, slow aging and improve overall health.

Antioxidants vs. Free Radicals

If you are already familiar with the scientific basis of antioxidants you can skip this section. But if you've always found free radicals and antioxidants confusing, read on.

Cells, like everything else, are composed of many different types of molecules and molecules are made up of one or more atoms of one or more basic elements (like carbon, oxygen, etc.). They are joined by chemical bonds. As you might remember from high school science, atoms have a nucleus (center), neutrons (electrically neutral particles), protons (positively charged particles) and electrons (negatively charged particles). The number of protons in an atom's nucleus determines the number of electrons (negatively charged particles) you will find surrounding the atom. Electrons are involved in chemical reactions and are what holds atoms together to form molecules. Electrons surround, or "orbit" an atom in one or more "shells".

The innermost shell is full when it has two electrons. When the first shell is full, electrons begin to fill the second

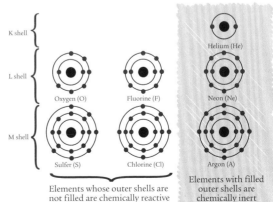

K shell

L shell

Oxygen (O)   Fluorine (F)

M shell

Sulfer (S)   Chlorine (Cl)

Helium (He)

Neon (Ne)

Argon (A)

Elements whose outer shells are not filled are chemically reactive

Elements with filled outer shells are chemically inert

shell. When the second shell has eight electrons, it is full, and so on. The number of electrons in an atom's outer shell is key to its chemical behavior. If it has a full outer shell is will not usually react chemically with other substances—it is stable or "inert". Atoms "want" to be stable and they will try to fill the outer shell with electrons by:

- gaining or losing electrons to fill or empty the outer shell
- sharing electrons by bonding together with other atoms (forming new molecules).

The number of electrons that are gained or lost is unique for each element, and this number determines how many different types of chemical bonds atoms of that element can form.

How Free Radicals are Formed
Normally, the bonds between electrons don't split and leave a molecule with an unpaired electron, but when bonds are weak it can happen and they *do* split. That's when free radicals are formed. Free radicals are very unstable and react quickly with other compounds, trying to capture the needed electron to gain stability. Generally, free radicals attack the nearest stable molecule, "stealing" an electron from it. When the "attacked" molecule loses its electron, it becomes a free radical, and a chain reaction begins that can damage living cells.

Some free radicals are necessary for life and some are created during normal metabolism. Sometimes our immune system will create free radicals on purpose to neutralize viruses and bacteria. Lifestyle and environmental factors, such as pollution, radiation, tobacco smoke, herbicides and pesticides can also cause the formation of free radicals.

Normally the body can handle free radicals. It has a number of mechanisms to minimize free radical damage and to repair damage that does occur, but if antioxidants are unavailable, or if free-radical production becomes excessive, cells will be disrupted.

Free radical damage accumulates with age and is thought to be a major factor in age-related diseases, conditions and in the speed of aging itself.

How Antioxidants Prevent Free Radical Damage

Antioxidants neutralize free radicals by donating one of their own electrons, ending the electron-"stealing" chain reaction. Antioxidant nutrients don't become free radicals by donating an electron because they are stable either way. They help prevent cell and tissue damage that can lead to health problems and disease.

Fresh berries, berry extracts and juices are excellent sources of antioxidant nutrients.

ORAC

The Oxygen Radical Absorbance Capacity, or ORAC value of foods, is a measurement of antioxidant levels. The higher the ORAC Value, the more antioxidant power a food has. Berry ORAC values top those of many other fruits and vegetables including oranges, grapefruit, cherries, plums, Brussels sprouts, broccoli and spinach. Blueberries, with an ORAC Value of 5486, have one of the highest antioxidant levels. Right behind are blackberries with an ORAC Value of 4654; strawberries at 3520 and raspberries, 2789.[8]

Blueberry

Blueberries — then and now

Records exist showing blueberries were used for medicinal purposes as far back as the 16th century, although "off the record" it is certain that natives of North America and Europe have been eating blueberries and using them as medicine since they first discovered these tasty little fruits. Whole berries, fresh, organically grown, are your best source of all the goodness of blueberries. However the limited growing season and high price of organic fruit don't have to be a deterrent in getting the best of the blueberries for your good health.

There are now highly concentrated juices and blueberry extracts that can provide much of the goodness of fresh berries and are as safe as fresh blueberries. A quality blueberry extract will be made from 100% fruit solids, skin, seeds, fibre and juice and have a high concentration. The most potent blueberry extract currently available is a 36:1 extract—that means that 36 grams of berries are concentrated to make one gram of potent extract.

Health Benefits

The small blueberry may be a BIG help in reducing age-related illness and health decline. Though blueberries are not a cure-all, they contain a variety of natural compounds which have health benefits. These substances include, but are not limited to fructose, fibre, vitamins and antioxidants. Antioxidants seem to have the most conclusive role in prevention and even treatment of such conditions and disease as cancer, heart disease and the aging process.

Scientific studies report blueberries may help:
- prevent urinary tract infections[9]
- slow aging and prevent cancer[10-16]
- reduce heart disease risk[17]
- lower cholesterol[17]
- strengthen collagen[18]
- regulate blood sugar[18]
- improve night vision[18]
- reduce replication of the HIV virus[19]
- treat diarrhea[18]

Heart Support
Rutgers and University of Wisconsin researchers are studying the ability of blueberry compounds to prevent platelet aggregation, a factor in heart disease. The compounds being studied appear to act in two ways. They seem to reduce oxidation of Low Density Lipoproteins ("bad" cholesterol), thus helping to lower arterial plaque build-up, and they reduce the stickiness of blood platelets helping to prevent the formation of blood clots.[17,20]

Cholesterol
A recent American Chemical Society meeting reported that a compound found in blueberries called *pterostilbene* has "the potential to be developed into a nutraceutical for lowering cholesterol, particularly for those who do not respond well to conventional drugs." The study's authors from the USDA's Agricultural Research Service said that the compound found in *Vaccinium* berries could be a "potent weapon in the battle against obesity and heart disease through its cholesterol-reducing potential." [17,20,21,22]

In fact it is not necessary to remove or isolate the healthy compounds of blueberries. A more holistic and no doubt less expensive option is to increase one's consumption of blueberries or to supplement with natural blueberry extracts!

Head researcher, Agnes M. Rimando and her associates "earlier showed that this compound may help fight cancer."An abstract of this study can be found on the USDA's Agricultural Research Service website.[22] According to the technical jargon of the research abstract, "These naturally occurring stilbenes, (compounds) known to be strong antioxidants and to have cancer chemopreventive activity, will add to purported health benefits derived from consumption of these small fruits."

The Eyes
Reports on the favorable effects of blueberries on eyesight include one study on Israeli fighter pilots.[23,24] They were given regular doses of blueberry and their night vision significantly improved. Blueberry compounds, with their high antioxidant capacity, seem to be able to enhance capillary elasticity and permeability of the tissues of the eye. A number of earlier studies in Europe have documented the relationship between bilberries, the European cousin of blueberries, and improved eyesight.

Wild blueberries are called "vision fruit" in Japan, because their high concentrations of anthocyanins, which are shown to reducing eyestrain as well as improving night vision. Blueberries are being studied for their potential to prevent macular degeneration, a disease of the retina and the leading cause of blindness in people over age 65.

The Brain
Research suggests that blueberries may protect against or help reverse nerve and brain-related conditions including forms of dementia, like Alzheimers disease.[25] According to a study conducted at the University of Guelph in Ontario, blueberries help protect the brain and central nervous system by increasing blood serum levels of antioxidants. Another Canadian study showed consumption of lowbush blueberries helped protect neurons in the brain against prolonged damage following a stroke.[26]

In a landmark study from Tufts University, 1999, old rats were fed the equivalent of 1 cup of blueberries per day in one month.[11] As a result of their diet change they learned faster than young rats, were more coordinated, showed improved motor skill and outperformed young rats in memory tests. What's more, only the animals consuming the blueberries also improved their balance and coordination, functions which tend to deteriorate as we get older. Technically speaking, the blueberries enhanced memory-associated neuron signaling and other neuron activity in the rats — activity that may help overcome a genetic predisposition to Alzheimers or Parkinsons disease. If one wants to win "the rat race" perhaps blueberries can help!

These findings are increasingly important as our population ages. Decreased cognitive and motor function that can accompany advanced age are a major fear for most people. Balanced, healthful nutrition and regular exercise — both mental and physical — are essential for us to enjoy all the years of our lives.

Antioxidant Power

ORAC is a rating system for antioxidant power. Scientists look at how all the different phytochemicals and antioxidants in a given food perform together and then give an overall rating to the food based on its performance. The ORAC rating identifies antioxidants in a given food and ranks how they work together and how much protection and value they provide when taken as a group in that particular food. Blueberries have one of the highest ORAC ratings of all foods.

Researchers at the USDA Human Nutrition Center found that blueberries rank #1 in antioxidant activity when compared to 40 other fresh fruits and vegetables.[27] Antioxidants help neutralize harmful by-products of metabolism called free radicals that can lead to cancer and other age related diseases. Anthocyanin, the pigment that makes the blueberries blue, is thought to be responsible for this major health benefit.

Urinary Tract Infections

Both blueberries and cranberries contain "epicatechin", a bioflavanoid that inhibits the binding of *E. coli* bacteria to the urinary tract wall.[9] Because it can't "stick", the bacteria is prevented from invading the tissues and causing an infection. Concentrated blueberry or cranberry extracts work quickly against infections and are excellent natural alternatives to antibiotics.

In Sweden, dried blueberries are used to treat childhood diarrhea (Kowalchuk, 1976). Their effectiveness is attributed to anthocyanosides, a natural substance found in blueberries which is believed to be lethal to *E. coli*, the bacteria sometimes linked to diarrheal infections.[28]

Blueberry Components

One serving of blueberries delivers the antioxidant power of 5 servings of most other fruits and vegetables.

Blueberries contain:
- anthocyanins and phenolics (antioxidants)
- lutein
- lignans
- gallic acid
- fibre
- vitamin C
- beta carotene
- vitamin E
- ellagic acid—ellagitannin
- folic acid

Safety

Although blueberries and their extracts are safe for everyone from children to seniors, the powerful natural effects of blueberries make it important to discuss supplementation with your health practitioner if you are using other medications, such as Warfarin®. Pregnant and nursing mothers should always check with their physician before changing their diet or supplementing.

Research Summaries

1. Journal of Agricultural and Food Chemistry 2004: Researchers isolated three compounds in blueberries known to lower cholesterol levels. In a follow-up study, one of the three phytochemicals—pterostilbene— showed a potent effect in stimulating a receptor protein in cells that is important in lowering cholesterol and other blood fats.

    Rimando AM, Kalt W, Magee JB, Dewey J, Ballington JR. Resveratrol, pterostilbene, and piceatannol in *vaccinium* berries. J Agric Food Chem. 2004 Jul 28;52(15):4713-9. [17]

2. In-vitro study in Biochemistry and Cell Biology: 24 hours of exposure to extracts of blueberry antioxidants sharply reduced the production of matrix metalloproteinases—enzymes that play a key role in the development (metastasis) of malignant tissue in human prostate cancer cells.

    Matchett MD, Mackinnon SL, Sweeney MI, Gottschall-Pass KT, Hurta RA. Blueberry flavonoids inhibit matrix metalloproteinase activity in DU145 human prostate cancer cells. Biochem Cell Biol. 2005 Oct;83(5):637-43. [81]

3. *Editor's note: We do not condone irradiating any living creatures, including rats. The research reported here may be of value if it protects animals and humans from the affects of radiation.*

    A team of researchers led by Barbara Shukitt-Hale studied a group of 60 young male rats by splitting them up into three groups.[14] The first group was fed a diet with no berries, the second was fed a diet with strawberry extract and the third group was fed a diet with blueberry extract. After the rats had been on the diets for two months, half of the rats were subjected to radiation to quicken the aging process. After half the rats were irradiated, the entire group was put through tests that included a maze test and a chemical test for dopamine. Low levels of dopamine point to poor memory and attention, and other poor mental skills.

The researchers found that the rats that had been irradiated and were on a diet with no berries performed the worst in the maze of the three groups, and also tested the lowest for dopamine levels. The rats that had been irradiated and were on a diet with berry extract performed as well as the group that had not been irradiated.

"What this cruel experiment seems to indicate," explained Mike Adams, a consumer health advocate and holistic nutritionist, "is that the natural medicines found in berries, including antioxidants and other phytonutrients, substantially protect the nervous system from radiation damage. This helps explain why people who follow poor nutritional habits get sunburned so easily," he added. "The study also indicates that berries can even help protect lab animals from researchers intent on harming them via inhumane medical experiments."

Cranberry

The Beautiful Cranberry

Cranberries are *"Vaccinium"* berries, related to blueberries, billberries and huckleberries. They have been used as food by Native Americans for centuries. Cranberries grow on low shrubs or vines that creep along the bottoms of bogs. Their dark pink flowers turn into berries that are first white and then deep red once ripe. Although they look delicious, the berries are extremely tart and for many years they were mostly used in jellies, sauces or other mixtures with sweeteners added. Since the early 1960s, new products, such as cranberry juices, mixed juices, dried berries (or "craisins") and supplemental berry powders and extracts have been developed, ensuring that people can get the benefits of cranberry all year round.

Nutritionally cranberries are a good source of vitamin C, vitamin A, potassium and fibre. They contain about 88 percent distilled water and are low in calories: 1 cup contains only 55 calories. Fresh cranberries contain high amounts of organic acids and various other phytonutrients. They also contain something called hippuric acid, which has antibacterial and natural antibiotic effects. Cranberries are loaded with bioflavanoids, which provide antioxidant protection. Research in Europe has specifically shown that the bioflavonoid anthocyanin, aids the formation of visual purple, a purplish red pigment contained in the retina of human eyes that is instrumental in colour and night vision.[24,30]

Cranberries are now grown commercially on approximately 35,000 acres in the United States and are a profitable crop in Canada, Latvia, and Poland.

It is suggested that cranberries became connected with Thanksgiving turkey when they were introduced to early American settlers by the Indians in Massachusetts in the 1600s.

Health Benefits

Cranberries and cranberry products offer several important health benefits. Many women already know what science continues to prove – cranberries can prevent and relieve bladder and urinary tract infections (UTIs). Many studies have indicated that cranberries exert an "anti-adhesion" effect on certain bacteria so they cannot stick to the walls of the urinary tract and spread infection.[31-49] Anyone who is required to use a catheter can benefit from the use of cranberry, as they may be prone to UTIs. Research suggests that cranberries may help protect our health in other ways, such as reducing risk of gum disease, ulcers, heart disease, and cancer.

With their high concentrations of vitamins, minerals, organic acids and other phytonutrients, cranberries can be used to prevent a variety of non-optimum health conditions, safely and naturally. A study conducted at Cornell University tested the antioxidant and antiproliferative potential of common fruits and found cranberries had the highest total phenolic content, total antioxidant activity and antiproliferative effects in human liver-cancer cells.[88]

Bladder & Urinary Tract Infections

80 percent of women will have one UTI in their adult life. Those over 65 have at least one infection *per year*. Aging males are also affected by UTIs which can cause painful and urgent urination. A Harvard research study, published in the Journal of American Medical Association, showed that women who drink cranberry juice have a 42% decrease in the risk of bladder infection. The study showed that components of cranberry juice prevent *E. coli* bacteria from adhering to the lining of the bladder and urethra, and help stop new bacteria from growing and multiplying in the urinary tract. Instead of forming colonies, the bacteria are flushed out through the urine. [31,34,48]

In another study cranberry juice cocktail was shown to have beneficial effects in 73% of patients tested with active urinary tract infections. (44 women and 16 men drank 16 oz of cranberry juice a day.) Bladder infections are most common in older women but also occur in men, younger women and in children. Chances of developing an infection can be increased by incontinence, pregnancy, sexual intercourse and use of a diaphragm or catheter, or immune disorders or diabetes.[32,36,44]

Cranberries also act as a prebiotic, promoting the growth of beneficial lactobacillus bacteria while inhibiting the growth of harmful *E. coli* and listeria.

The Brain

Using an animal model James Joseph, PhD and Barbara Shukitt-Hale, PhD have been experimenting with cranberries and their ability to protect brain cells from free radical damage and subsequent motor and cognitive function losses. Rats fed diets supplemented with cranberries are put through a series of tests to evaluate their neural function compared to a control group. Preliminary results indicate that there will be compelling evidence that cranberry can help protect the brain from neurological damage (unpublished results).[29]

Anti-cancer

Laboratory studies conducted by University of Illinois scientists and published in *Planta Medica* showed potential anti-carcinogenic properties of cranberries.[50]

Preliminary results of a new study on mice, conducted at the University of Western Ontario, found that eating cranberries cut their risk of breast cancer. Three groups of mice were injected with human breast cancer cells. One group was fed dehydrated cranberries with their food, the second group had cranberry juice in place of their water, and the third group had no cranberry supplement. 40% percent fewer tumours than expected were noted in the mice that received cranberry juice, while the mice fed dehydrated cranberries had HALF the number of tumours found in the control group. The cranberry supplements prevented the cells from growing, metastasizing and spreading to the lungs and lymph nodes.

Laboratory studies have also shown positive effects in combating colon cancer because of a flavanoid called quercetin, found in cranberries.[51] Although these results are very preliminary, compounds in cranberries may prove to be a potent cancer fighter.

Anti-aging

The same research program that showed blueberries' capacity for improving neural activity and motor skills in aging mice also investigated cranberries and found they were equally effective in protecting brain cells from free radical damage. Rats feed diets supplemented with cranberries were put through a series of tests to evaluate neural function compared to a control group. Preliminary results indicate that cranberry can very likely help protect the brain from neurological damage (unpublished results).[29]

Dental Health

Soon you may find yourself brushing your teeth with cranberry compounds! *Critical Reviews in Food Science and Nutrition* (2002) reported on a preliminary clinical trial using a mouthwash containing cranberry material.[52] Saliva samples of the experimental group showed a significant reduction in Streptococcus (S. mutans) bacteria compared with the placebo group (unpublished data). A large percentage of dental caries (cavities) can be attributed to *S. mutans*. Dental plaque is mostly composed of bacteria that have attached themselves to tooth and gum surfaces, and to each other. Plaque is a major cause of periodontal disease. If cranberry can exert its anti-adhesion ability on teeth it will be a major advance in dental health.

Heart Health

Cranberries contain flavonoids and polyphenolic compounds that have been shown to inhibit the oxidation of "bad cholesterol", low density lipoprotein (LDL).[53, 54, 55] continuing research into this aspect of cranberry antioxidant action suggests that cranberries may offer a natural defense against atherosclerosis. In one study, 21 men in a 14-day trial drank 7 mL/kg body weight of cranberry juice per day. Short-term cranberry juice supplementation resulted in a significant increase in their plasma antioxidant capacity and a reduction in circulating oxidized LDL.

Stomach Ulcers

Current research is suggesting that a bacterium called *Helicobacter pylori*, or *H. pylori*, may be the primary cause of peptic ulcers.[56] In much the same way as cranberry can prevent *E. coli* from attaching itself to the urinary tract walls, specific constituents of cranberry have been shown to inhibit the adhesion of *H. pylori* to the mucus and lining of the digestive tract. Preliminary results suggest that cranberry could help prevent peptic ulcers.

Cranberry Components

Vitamins:
- vitamin A (beta-carotene)
- vitamin B1 (thiamine)
- vitamin B2 (riboflavin)
- vitamin B3 (niacin)
- vitamin B5 (pantothenic acid)
- vitamin B6 (pyridoxine)
- folacin (folic acid)
- vitamin C (ascorbic acid)
- vitamin E (alpha-tocopherol)

Minerals:
- boron
- calcium
- chromium
- copper
- iron
- magnesium
- manganese
- molybdenum
- phosphorous
- potassium
- selenium
- sodium
- sulfur

Organic Acids
One of the distinguishing aspects of cranberry, particularly in comparison with other berries in the same family, is its high organic acid level. Organic acids in cranberries act as a preservative and antifungal agent, keeping them fresh for a very long time. The main organic acids in cranberry are malic acid, quinic and citric acids. All of these have some health benefits.

Phytonutrients
Cranberries contain a wide variety of phytonutrients, the biologically active substances in plants that give them color, flavour and natural resistance to disease. Researchers around the world have been working

to isolate specific phytonutrients that can help in prevention of disease and improvement of various other health conditions.

The cranberry contains many of recently discovered and well-known phytonutrients:

- anthocyanins
- catechins
- chlorogenic acid
- eugenol
- lutein
- proanthocyanidins
- quercetin

Safety

Cranberries and their products are exceedingly safe. Pregnant and nursing mothers should discuss supplementation and nutritional changes with their physician.

Patients taking Warfarin® (also brand names Coumadin®, Jantoven®, Marevan®, and Waran®) or other anticoagulant or blood thinning pharmaceuticals should not drink cranberry juice as it may increase the drug's effectiveness.

Research Summaries

1. Tel Aviv University researchers describe the anti-*E. coli* adherence property of cranberry juice and attempt to identify the specific components in cranberries that cause this beneficial effect. They conclude that a compound in cranberries prevents certain *E. coli* from adhering to the bladder's lining. Orange, pineapple, mango, guava and grapefruit juices did not possess this anti-adhesion property.[36]

2. Harvard Medical School researchers conduct a large-scale clinical trial to demonstrate that drinking cranberry juice cocktail regularly, significantly reduced the presence of bacteria in the urine. Researchers found there was something specific in cranberry that prevented bacteria from adhering to the urinary tract. This research was conducted with 153 women, average age of 78, using 10 ounces of a cranberry juice cocktail, which contained 27 percent cranberry juice.[31]

3. In a small, double-blind clinical trial, researchers from Weber State University found that sexually active women between the ages of 18 and 45 who daily consume a cranberry dietary supplement for six months had a significantly lower risk of UTIs than women taking a placebo.[32]

4. Rutgers-led scientists identify the active components in cranberries responsible for maintaining urinary tract health as proanthocyanidins or condensed tannins. The researchers concluded that the cranberry *Vaccinium* proanthocyanidins in cranberry juice are responsible for promoting urinary tract health.[37]

5. Research led by Rutgers University researchers presented at Experimental Biology 2001 confirms that cranberry *Vaccinium* proanthocyanidins are absorbed in the body. This suggests that once cranberry proanthocyanidins are absorbed into the bloodstream they become available to other sites throughout the body and may function as anti-adhesion agents and/or antioxidants.[38]

6. Researchers from the Rutgers and the University of Wisconsin investigated the anti-adhesion effects of cranberry juice cocktail versus other foods that contain proanthocyanidins (PACs). In this human study, they found that only consumption of cranberry juice cocktail

resulted in urine with microbial anti-adhesion activity. Grape and apple juices, green tea and chocolate were also tested and did not produce this anti-adhesion activity.[48]

7. A University of British Columbia urologist found use of cranberry juice and tablets with increased fluid intake are more effective than fluids alone in preventing UTIs in women studied. Forty percent fewer women experienced UTIs when receiving cranberry products vs. placebo, and on average had half the number of UTIs.[34]

8. Findings by researchers suggest that regular consumption of cranberry juice cocktail may offer protection against certain antibiotic resistant bacteria that cause urinary tract infections (UTIs). This research, conducted by Rutgers and the University of Michigan, suggests that regular consumption of cranberry juice cocktail could reduce potential development of UTIs, thus decreasing the rate of antibiotic resistance.[44]

Cranberries, Cranberry Juice or Extracts?

Natural health experts and naturopathic doctors have been recommending cranberry for years. As many people are concerned about excess sugar and carbohydrate intake, fresh cranberries, dried berries, natural unsweetened cranberry juice, or concentrated cranberry extracts are a better choice for most people than the commercial, high sugar cranberry "cocktail" drinks. Cranberry extract capsules have added convenience when you are traveling or at work or school.

One of the most recommended ways to get the health benefits of Cranberry is in a 36:1 extract (36 grams of cranberries go into every gram of concentrated extract). Using cranberry fruit grown and harvested in the lower mainland of British Columbia, Canada, without pesticides or herbicides, this concentrated extract uses 100% of the fruit including fruit solids, skins, seeds, fibre and juice. By choosing this sort of highly potent extract you are sure of getting ALL the cranberry goodness with no added sugars, preservatives, flavours, colours or water.

"Cranberry Juice is the best herbal remedy for bladder infections. Purchase pure, unsweetened juice. If pure juice is not available, cranberry capsules can be substituted. Always take these with a large glass of water. Avoid cranberry juice cocktail products. These contain relatively little pure cranberry juice (less than 30% in some cases) and have high-fructose corn-syrup or other sweeteners added."[57]

"Cranberry juice, well-accepted as a folk remedy for the problem, also has held up under scientific scrutiny. Cranberry juice — at least the ordinary variety — is full of sugar and water, with only some of the real juice. The high sugar content may actually encourage the growth of bacteria and yeast. So my preference is to drink unsweetened cranberry juice concentrate, which you can buy in a health-food store, or to buy cranberry capsules. Take two capsules twice a day. Even if you're taking pharmaceutical drugs to treat the infection, I'd still take cranberry along with them." — *Dr. Andrew Weil*

Pomegranate

A Long History of Health

Sales of pomegranate juice have sky-rocketed due to media articles about this antioxidant-rich fruit linked to improved heart health, cancer prevention and arthritis relief.

The pomegranate may not look like the berries we have been discussing elsewhere, but it is technically a berry—a many-seeded "ovary" or seed pod surrounded by a fleshy outer layer. Pomegranates used to be relatively unknown in North American markets, although garnet-coloured pomegranate juice is a popular drink in the Middle East, and is the fruit and seeds are used extensively in Middle Eastern and Indian cuisine. In Greece and Turkey pomegranate is used in many recipes from salads to marinades and glazes, relishes, liqueurs and desserts.

The name pomegranate comes from Latin *pomum* for apple and *granatus* for seeded. Both Grenada, an island nation, and the hand grenade got their names from this fruit, called "la grenade" in French. Grenadine syrup, used in mixing cocktails, is thickened, sweetened pomegranate juice. The pomegranate has a long history as an element of myths, legends and art through the ages, from ancient Egypt to modern times.

In Greek mythology the pomegranate is a central element of the story of why we have seasons of the year. Persephone was the daughter of Demeter, Goddess of the Harvest. Hades took Persephone, against her will, to live with him in the Underworld. Demeter went into mourning for her lost daughter and all the green plants of earth ceased to grow. Zeus (the "head god") commanded Hades to return Persephone, however there was a "rule" that anyone who consumed food or drink in the Underworld was doomed to spend eternity there. Although Persphone had eaten nothing else, Hades tricked her into eating six pomegranate seeds while she was still his prisoner. This condemned her to spend six months of each year in the Underworld and, according to the legend, those six months are our Fall and Winter.

The pomegranate is probably one of the most difficult berries to eat! You must open the leathery skin with a knife, break it open and remove the "arils" or seeds and separate them from the white material that surrounds them in sections. The entire seed can be eaten raw, though the juicy outer part of the seed where all the flavour is. Different varieties of pomegranate range in flavour from very sweet to tangy or very sour and bitter, with a characteristic "dry" taste from the tannins in the fruit.

Health Benefits

One pomegranate delivers 40% of an adult's daily vitamin C requirement. It is also a rich source of folic acid and of antioxidants. Pomegranates are high in polyphenols. The most abundant of these are tannins, particularly a group called "punicalagins", which appear to be the antioxidant responsible for the potent free-radical scavenging ability of pomegranate. Its tannin content has effects similar to that of green tea, and significantly greater than that of red wine.

Pomegranate seeds possess anti-inflammatory properties by inhibiting some of the enzymes responsible for inflammation. (Chronic inflammation has been linked to the incidence of many types of cancer.)[58]

Many food and supplement producers use pomegranate extracts instead of the juice. The extract has no sugar, calories, or additives, but retains the health benefits of the juice and can be used year-round with great convenience. The fruit's antioxidant constituents are rapidly absorbed by the body and are non-toxic.

Pomegranate Components

Pomegranates contain:
- vitamin C
- tannins — punicalagins
- ellagic acid

Actions:
- antioxidant
- anti-inflammatory
- cancer preventive
- blood pressure improvement
- heart health support

Research Summaries

1. A University of California study involved 46 men with recurrent prostate cancer and rising PSA levels after surgery or radiotherapy. PSA levels are measure a specific antigen and can show if cancer is progressing or not. PSA levels were checked prior to the trial enabling the researchers to calculate the time for PSA levels to double. Short doubling times indicate that the person is more likely to die from cancer. After taking 8oz of pomegranate juice, 570 mg polyphenols daily for 3 months, the average doubling time increased from 15 months to 54 months. This shows a significant reduction in the speed of cancer progress. In vitro tests of the subjects before and after showed a 12% decrease in spread of the cancer and a 17% increase in apoptosis. The results may be due to an anti-inflammatory effect. Chronic inflammation has been linked to the incidence of many cancers.

2. In 2005, researchers at the University of Wisconsin tested various doses of pomegranate extract on human prostate cancer cells in the lab. The higher the dose of the extract, the more cancer cells died. Then, in tests with mice that were injected with human prostate cancer cells, the animals that received the highest concentration of pomegranate extract had the least progression of prostate cancer and declining levels of prostate specific antigen (PSA), a marker for prostate cancer in humans. In a comparison group of mice that received only water instead of pomegranate extract, tumors grew much faster.

3. Pomegranate juice offers protection against cardiovascular disease. Scientific studies have shown that it does this by reducing the oxidation and accumulation of LDL, the "bad"cholesterol and by reducing systolic blood pressure. An extract of pomegranate was also tested and showed a reduction of harmful products of lipid (fat) oxidation in diabetic patients, without affecting their insulin levels.[60,61,62,63,64]

4. A 2004 study in Clinical Nutrition found that 19 patients with severe atherosclerosis of the carotid arteries who drank 2 ounces of pomegranate juice daily for three years showed remarkable improvement. Ultrasound tests showed that narrowing of the arteries decreased by 35% on average in the pomegranate group, while the condition worsened by nearly 10% in the control group. The average systolic blood pressure was also significantly lowered in the group that drank pomegranate juice.

5. Pomegranate juice extract has also been found to improve signs of clinical gum disease, which is considered to be a precursor and/or indication of cardiovascular disease.

6. Diabetes is associated with increased oxidative stress and the development of atherosclerosis. Professor Michael Aviram and researchers at the Rambam Medical Center in Haifa, Israel, looked at the effects of pomegranate juice on diabetic blood parameters and oxidative stress levels in diabetic patients.

   "In most juices, sugars are present in free – and harmful – forms," explained Aviram. "In pomegranate juice, however, the sugars are attached to unique antioxidants, which actually make these sugars protective against atherosclerosis."

   Published in the Atherosclerosis journal (Vol. 187, pp. 363–371), the study reports that subjects who drank 50 ml of pomegranate juice (containing 1.5 millimoles of polyphenols) every day for three months experienced a reduced risk for atherosclerosis.[67] The juice contained 1979 mg of tannins, 384 mg of anthocyanins, and 121 mg of ellagic acid derivatives per litre.

   Ten type-2 diabetics and 10 healthy control subjects participated and after three months researchers found that the pomegranate juice consumption did not affect blood levels of glucose, cholesterol or triglycerides, it *did* significantly reduce serum lipid peroxides and oxidation of LDL cholesterol levels by 56 and 28 per cent respectively. Oxidation of the LDL-cholesterol has been reported to be a major contributor to atherosclerosis, and thus heart disease risk.

7. According to a Case Western Reserve University School of Medicine study published in the September 2005 issue of the *Journal of Nutrition*, pomegranate fruit extracts can block enzymes that contribute to osteoarthritis.[69] The study showed the ability of a pomegranate extract to inhibit a pro-inflammatory protein molecule that contributes to cartilage destruction in osteoarthritic patients. The Case study demonstrated for the first time the ability of pomegranate extracts to slow the deterioration of human cartilage.

Blackberry & Raspberry

The Aggregate Fruits

Blackberries and raspberries are called "aggregate fruits" because each berry is really a cluster of tiny fruits, called druplets, and each druplet contains a seed. There are many relatives in the Blackberry/Raspberry families including dewberries, thimbleberries and the European "Rubus fructosus" or brambleberry. These berries are relatives of the rose—hence the painfully effective thorns! Their soft, juicy fruit is well-protected by thorny bushes or trailing vines. They are also sometimes called "cane berries" because of the way they grow on stiff offshoots.

The blackberry is a very hardy plant that has been around a very long time. It was prescribed by the Greeks for gout. Blackberries are mentioned in the Bible and in other early writings, especially in Britain. The raspberry is known for its sweet but slightly tart berries. Both have now been shown to offer antioxidant benefits and other health support. Studies reveal substances that may help prevent cancer, reduce heart disease, ease inflammation, protect against age-related macular degeneration, and prevent overgrowth of some bacteria, fungi and infections such as *Candida albicans*.

Blackberries have a high tannin content. Tannins are substances in the seeds and stems of grapes, the bark of some trees, tea leaves and some berries. They are astringent, which means they tend to draw together or constrict tissues. The result of eating something astringent is a dryness in the mouth. They serve a plant by counteracting bacteria and fungal invaders by interfering with their surface proteins.

Harold McGee, who wrote "On Foods & Cooking", describes astringency, caused by tannins, as "that dry, puckery, constricting sensation that follows on a sip of strong tea or an assertive red wine, or a bite into less than ripe fruit."

Tannins are essential to the development of both flavours and colours in fruits and in wine or tea.

Unfortunately these aggregate berries can turn very soft and mushy and grow mouldy very quickly. They are best used the same day they are picked or purchased, or they can be frozen. Due to the fact that they have limited seasons, and with growing interest in their therapeutic value, science has developed ways to capture all the key phytochemicals and nutrients of blackberries and raspberries in concentrates and extracts. Although these dietary supplements can't be sprinkled on ice cream or baked in a pie, new technologies give us a convenient way to get "berry goodness" year round.

Health Benefits

Blackberries and black raspberries contain an extremely dark pigment which gives them one of the highest antioxidant ratings in fruits and berries. Rich in ellagic acid, anthocyanins and antioxidants, black raspberries have been called the "king of berries" for their superior health benefits. They can contribute to better immunity and protection from disease as well as helping us slow the aging process. The combination of anthocyanins, Vitamin C, and ellagic acid in these berries are combined to give them a high ORAC (Oxygen Radical Absorbance Capacity) rating.

Blackberries and Raspberries help:
- ease minor infections
- treat hemorroids (because of their high tannin content)
- lessen minor bleeding
- alleviate diarrhea
- ease intestinal inflammation
- improve health as antioxidants

German health practitioners often recommend blackberries for mild infections such as sore throats and mouth irritations. Scientists have reported anti-tumor properties associated with the tannins found in some varieties of berries.

Blackberries/Raspberries Components

Blackberries and Raspberries contain:
- antioxidants, such as anthocyanin pigments
- vitamin C
- vitamin E
- ellagic acid
- salicylate, an active substance found in aspirin
- insoluble fibre
- soluble fibre, such as pectin.
- manganese
- magnesium
- niacin
- riboflavin
- folate
- gallic acid, rutin
- quercetin
- catechins
- potassium
- copper

As well as being a rich source of healthful phytochemicals, blackberries and raspberries are low on the glycemic index, making them an ideal fruit for those with diabetes, metabolic syndrome or other blood sugar challenges. The ORAC level of black raspberries is 77 µmoles /TE/g, a very powerful antioxidant.

Ellagic Acid

Ellagic Acid is a compound abundant in red raspberries and pomegranates. Ellagic acid research suggests that this nutrient could have profound anti-cancer effects. Ellagic acid has been shown to inhibit certain important cellular "receptors" known to be cancer "growth factors". This action of ellagic acid "may be helpful for the prevention and treatment of cancer."[71]

European Urology reported on another positive effect of ellagic acid for men undergoing chemotherapy for prostate cancer. It appears that ellagic acid reduced some of the toxic effects of chemotherapy, especially the low white cell count. "Our study suggests that the use of ellagic acid as support therapy reduces chemotherapy induced toxicity…"[72]

Anthocyanins
Raspberries and blackberries are rich in anthocyanins, the flavonoids that give them their red and purple colours. Anthocyanins act as anti-inflammatory compounds and can protect both large and small blood vessels from oxidative damage.

Inflammation and pain and swelling, go hand in hand. Enzymes involved in inflammation can damage connective tissue in capillaries, and blood can leak into surrounding tissues. Oxidants (free radicals) are released and further damage capillary walls. Anthocyanins can neutralize the enzymes that destroy connective tissue. They can neutralize the oxidants and prevent tissue damage, and they can help repair the damaged proteins of the blood-vessel walls. Animal experiments showed that supplementing with concentrated anthocyanins, such as blueberry, blackberry and raspberry concentrates, can help prevent or reduce inflammation and minimize capillary damage.[73]

Anthocyanins have been studied for their anti-cancer effects. One *in vitro* study showed that anthocyanins suppressed the growth of colon cancer cells. This study also found that some anthocyanins were effective at 1/10 the concentration of genistein, an anti-carcinogenic plant estrogen from soy.[74]

Quercetin
Quercetin is a flavonoid found in red raspberries and other fruits. It has been shown to reduce allergic reactions, having an anti-histamine effect. It also helps reduce the peroxidation of LDL ("bad") cholesterol and it may help the body destroy cancer cells. Quercetin appears to induce a process, called 'apoptosis,' that is one of the primary ways the body eliminates damaged cells. Studies show that quercetin can induce apoptosis in colorectal and skin cancer cells. Additional research suggests that quercetin and ellagic acid work together to reduce cancer risk and promote apoptosis.[75]

Catechins
Catechins are flavonols that support the antioxidant defense system. Catechins found in red raspberries, just as those found in green tea, may contribute to cancer prevention. The catechin content of 100 grams of red raspberries (about 3/4 cup) is .83 milligrams.

Reducing Risk of Cancer. An extract from fresh blackberries was shown in research studies to reduce the size of cancerous tumours and prevent proliferation of cancer cells in animals. Fruits and vegetables have long been associated with a lower incidence of cancer, and their antioxidant activity has been the most likely reason. According to researchers from the US Agricultural Research Service and the National Institute for Occupational Safety and Health: *"Little is known about the active ingredients in these antioxidants and how these components exert their effects on the inhibition of cancer growth."*

The researchers, led by cell biologist Min Ding and plant physiologist Shiow Wang, identified a water-soluble flavonoid called "cyanidin-3-glucoside", C3G for short, as the active compound responsible for the antioxidant benefits of blackberries. Ding and Wang tested the anti-cancer Potential of C3G, and published their findings in the *Journal of Biological Chemistry* in June. (Vol. 281, Issue 25, 17359–17368).[79]

They first tested C3G on a group of mice with skin tumours. The mice that received the C3G supplement showed a significant reduction in the growth and spread of tumours compared to those that did not. They also looked at the effects of C3G in lung-cancer cells of immune-suppressed mice; lung cancer is more likely to spread to other organs than other forms of cancer. They observed that the C3G reduced the growth of cancer cells and their tendency to spread.

The researchers credited the antioxidant effect of the blackberry compound for these results, since free radicals can contribute to the development and spread of cancer. Reports suggest that this compound has been isolated and has a patent application pending, however the benefits can be realized without waiting for an isolated pharmaceutical compound. High potency berry concentrates can provide such nutrients made from 100% fruit solids and juice, combining the benefits of more than one isolated phytochemical.

Safety

Although raspberries are rich in health promoting phytochemicals and nutrients, they also contain considerable amounts of oxalates, substances that can interfere with the absorption of calcium. Persons with concerns about kidney or gall stones should check with their health care practitioner before eating large quantities of raspberries. It is recommended that you should take your calcium supplements 2 or 3 hours after eating raspberries to ensure proper calcium absorption.

Research Summaries

1. Studies at Ohio State University have found significant decreases in colon tumors in rats and esophageal tumors in mice fed a diet with black raspberries. In fact, an 80% reduction in esophageal cancers occurred in mice fed a 5-10% diet of black raspberries. In vitro studies have shown that extracts of raspberries and blackberries may slow the growth of breast cervical, colon and esophageal cancers. Human clinical trials are underway to assess the effects of black raspberries on colon and esophageal cancers in humans.[76,77,78]

2. Newborn mice treated with ellagic acid, after exposure to carcinogens, developed 44 to 75 percent fewer lung tumors than the control group. Topical application of ellagic acid reduced the number of skin tumors in mice exposed to known carcinogens by 59 to 66 percent compared to controls.[70] (*Editor's note: Again, we do not condone animal testing. We are only encouraged that natural means for cancer prevention or treatment may become nearer to reality as a result of these trials*).

Strawberry

Strawberries in History

The earliest mention of the strawberry in English language writings is in a Saxon plant list of the tenth century. In 1265 the "straberie" is mentioned. Although many people think the word "strawberry" comes from the practice of placing straw under the cultivated plants when the berries are ripening, the name predates such a custom. More likely 'straw' is related to the verb "to strew" as strawberry stringers, vine-like stems, appear to be strewn across the ground. Related to the rose, strawberries are not true botanical berries, but they certainly match our common understanding of a berry as a small tasty fruit.

The strawberry is a member of the rose family that has been known, and loved by many, for centuries. Strawberries are an excellent source of vitamin C and also provide some potassium and iron. They were used as far back as Roman times for healing and prevention of fever, gout, bad breath, a sore throat and fainting. Modern science is providing insight into why and how strawberries can enhance health.

Health Benefits

Strawberries have laxative, diuretic and astringent properties. Both leaves and berries have been used by healers over the centuries.

Strawberries and strawberry extracts have been used for:
- reducing fevers
- easing digestive difficulties, diarrhea and dysentery
- treating rheumatic gout

The root of the strawberry plant is astringent and has been used for diarrhea, while strawberry leaf tea provides a treatment for dysentery.

New research shows that a component of strawberries could also enhance memory. Pamela Maher, Ph.D., of the Cellular Neurobiology Laboratory at the Salk Institute, lead researcher in one study, explains, "This is the first time that the function of a defined natural product has been characterized at the molecular level in the central nervous system and shown to enhance long-term memory. The good news is that fisetin is readily available in strawberries. The bad news is that, because of its natural product status, there may be little financial interest in getting it into human clinical trials for diseases associated with memory loss such as Alzheimer's, where the treatment options are currently very limited."

While eating strawberries sounds enjoyable, Maher cautions that it would take about 10 pounds a day to achieve a beneficial effect. However new, high potency fruit extracts make it easier to increase our intake of the health enhancing phytochemical compounds found in strawberries.

· ·
- Strawberries are the only fruit that grows seeds on the outside.
- There are over 200 seeds on every strawberry.
- 12 ounces of strawberries = 97 calories if no sugar is added. Great food for diets.
- Iroquois Indians grew strawberries as one of their most important crops.
- Eight strawberries contain more Vitamin C than a medium sized orange.
· ·

Strawberry Components

Strawberries contain:
- malic acid
- citric acids
- natural sugar
- pectin
- fibre

Research Summary

1. According to recent research from the Salk Institute for Biological Studies, a naturally occurring flavonoid commonly found in strawberries, called fisetin, can stimulate signaling pathways in the brain that enhance long-term memory.[81]

2. Lead researcher author, Pamela Maher, Ph.D., of the Cellular Neurobiology Laboratory at the Salk Institute explains, "Fisetin compounds induce differentiation or maturation of neural cells," Maher explains, "This suggested to us that these compounds might not only protect neural cells from dying but might promote new connections between nerve cells."

3. Maher, and co-authors Tatsuhiro Akaishi and Kazuho Abe, at Musashino University in Tokyo, Japan, extended their initial study and found that fisetin protects and promotes survival of cultured neurons and boosts memory in healthy mice. This makes it a promising candidate for further study.

Cherry

Ah, the delicious cherry! One of the first fruits of summer, and unfortunately one with a very short season. There are a wide variety of cherries—more than 1000 varieties of sweet cherries alone—and even though they don't qualify as "berries" technically, they are similar in nutritional profile. Cherries are actually related to plums, peaches, almonds, and apricots. Bing cherries, Rainier, Queen Anne and Marachino are among the best known of the sweet cherries. Tart cherries are often referred to as pie cherries or sour cherries and they are generally canned or frozen for use throughout the year. The most common tart cherry variety is the Montorency, deep red and perfect for pies, cobblers, turnovers, preserves and jams.

Cherries appear to have originated in a number of different countries around the world, from Italy, Greece, Spain, France and also from China. Cherries have been grown in North American since the early 1600s and they are a popular crop in both eastern and western Canada and the US.

Decorative cherry tree varieties can make neighbourhoods beautiful in Spring, but do not produce edible fruit.

Health Benefits

Cherries can help:
- relieve joint pain and inflammation
- support immunity
- improve sleep
- build healthy blood
- treat gout

Like all the other bright coloured fruits and berries we have been discussing, cherries contain anthocyanins are potent antioxidants, supporting the immune system and heart health. Cherries or cherry extracts may also help improve sleep as they contain high levels of melatonin, a natural nutrient that helps re-set the body's clock.

There are many pharmaceutical medications sold as "COX-2 inhibitors" to reduce joint pain and inflammation, but if cherries, with their high levels of melatonin, may be a much safer option than Non-Steroidal Anti-Inflammatory drugs (NSAIDs). NSAIDs can cause considerable pain and damage to the digestive tract.

Cherries are especially high in potassium and Vitamin C, and low in fat and sodium. They also contain calcium, phosphorus, copper and iron, important for building healthy blood.

Research Summary

1. The antioxidant melatonin was recently identified in a variety of edible plants and seeds in high concentrations.[82] In plants, as in animals, melatonin is believed to function as a free radical scavenger. In this study, melatonin was detected and quantified in fresh-frozen tart cherries (Prunus cerasus) using high-performance liquid chromatography. Both cherry species contain high levels of melatonin compared to the melatonin concentrations in the blood of mammals. Montmorency cherries (13.46 ± 1.10 ng/g) contain ˜6 times more melatonin than do Balaton cherries (2.06 ± 0.17 ng/g). Neither the orchard of origin nor the time of harvest influenced the amount of melatonin in fresh cherries. The implication of the current findings is that cherries could be an important source of dietary melatonin.

Cherry

Elderberry

The Elderberry, which can produce red, bluish or black berries, has a long history of use as a medicinal plant. The flowers, leaves, berries, bark and roots have all been used in traditional folk medicine for centuries, giving elderberry the nickname, "the medicine chest of the common people". Because various parts of the plant are used it is sometimes just called "elder".

Early research showed that elderberry jam contains many vitamins and minerals, including vitamin B17, also called laetrile. This nutrient, given vitamin status in 1952, is prevalent in the seeds of fruits of the Prunus Rosacea family (bitter almond, apricot, blackthorn, elderberry, cherry, nectarine, peach and plum). It has been shown to have anti-cancer properties.[83]

Elderflower Water was a constant companion on our great-grandmothers' vanity, as it was used to improve the complexion, keeping it fair and free from blemishes or freckles.

Health Benefits

Elderberry apparently stimulates and strengthens the immune system, while directly inhibiting the influenza (flu) virus. Interestingly, elderberry contains an enzyme that smoothes down the pointed spikes on the outside of the virus, so it cannot pierce through cell walls. This is why elderberry syrups are popular flu remedies.

Elderberry extract has also been shown to:
- fight inflammation
- lower fever
- stimulate circulation
- soothe the respiratory tract
- improve urinary complaints
- reduce edema (swelling)
- ease muscle pain
- provide antibiotic, antiviral and antibacterial support.

Elderberry is diaphoretic — that means it makes you sweat. In this way it helps eliminate waste in the fluid surrounding the blood cells. Elder flowers and elder flower water have been used in a variety of ways topically and as a tonic mixture. Elder flowers are a mild astringent and are used in skin washes to refine the complexion and help relieve eczema, acne and psoriasis.

Elderberry Components

Elderberries contain:
- potassium
- viburnic acid (useful for asthma an bronchitis)
- vitamin A
- vitamin B
- vitamin C (more vitamin C than any other herb except for black currants and rosehips!)
- bioflavonoids.[83]
- quercetin
- tannins
- amino acids

Taken at the first sign of cold or flu, Elderberry can often reduce the course of the infection.[84,85] It supports the immune system, offering the body additional amounts of vitamin C, fruit acids and essential oils and anthocyanidins. Warm elderberry wine has been used as a remedy for sore throat and influenza and to induce perspiration to reverse the effects of a chill. The juice from the berries is an old-fashioned cure for colds and to relieve asthma and bronchitis.

Safety

Raw berries have laxative and diuretic properties, however the seeds are toxic and may induce vomiting and nausea. Elderberries should be cooked.

Research Summaries

1. Randomized study of the efficacy and safety of oral elderberry extract in the treatment of influenza A and B virus infections. *J Int Med Res. 2004 Mar-Apr;32(2):132–40.*

Elderberry has been used in folk medicine for centuries to treat influenza, colds and sinusitis, and has been reported to have antiviral activity against influenza and herpes simplex. The efficacy and safety of oral elderberry syrup was tested for treating influenza A and B infections. Sixty patients (aged 18–54 years) suffering from influenza-like symptoms for 48 h or less were enrolled in this randomized, double-blind, placebo-controlled study during the influenza season of 1999–2000 in Norway. Patients received 15 ml of elderberry or placebo syrup four times a day for 5 days, and recorded their symptoms using a visual analogue scale. Symptoms were relieved on average 4 days earlier and use of rescue medication was significantly less in those receiving elderberry extract compared with placebo.

2. Incorporation of the elderberry anthocyanins by endothelial cells increases protection against oxidative stress. *Free Radic Biol Med. 2000 Jul 1;29(1):51–60.*

The objective of this study was to investigate the ability of endothelial cells (EC) to incorporate anthocyanins and to examine their potential benefits against various oxidative stressors. Endothelial dysfunction has been proposed to play an important role in the initiation and development of vascular disease, with studies having shown that administration of antioxidants improves endothelial function. Elderberry anthocyanins, where incorporated into the plasma membrane of EC. The enrichment of EC with elderberry anthocyanins conferred significant protective effects in EC against oxidative stressors: hydrogen peroxide, dihydrochloride and ascorbic acid. These results show for the first time that vascular EC can incorporate anthocyanins into the membrane, conferring significant protective effects against oxidative insult. These findings may have important implications on preserving EC function and preventing the initiation of EC changes associated with vascular diseases.[85]

Black Currant

In the United Kingdom and elsewhere during World War II, fruits rich in vitamin C, such as oranges, became almost impossible to obtain. Blackcurrant berries however are a rich source of vitamin C and they grew well in the UK climate. The British government encouraged people to grow blackcurrants and much of the fruit was made into a syrup. This was mixed with water and provided free to children in the UK as blackcurrant cordial to ensure they had enough vitamin C in their diets. Blackcurrant flavouring, candies and jams are still popular in Britain and the juice has become known as a health-enhancing source of antioxidants and vitamins (much like pomegranate juice).

Health Benefits

Who would have thought that little blackcurrants could help prevent everything from Alzheimer's disease to cancer, from urinary tract infections to heart disease!

Black Currants can help:
· protect brain health
· increase antioxidant protection
· improve mood

Research Summaries

1. Researchers found that anthocyanins and polyphenolics in black currants had a strong protective effect in neuronal cells in laboratory trials (in vitro). 'These compounds also work in hippocampal cells taken straight from the brain," researcher James Joseph of Tufts University said, "The research suggests that these protective effects may be reproduced in the human body where they could help prevent or delay the onset of Alzheimer's." Earlier research showed the power of black currants as antioxidants, but this is the first study to demonstrate that they may help protect brain cells.

2. Recent studies show that black currants may effectively ward off the Staphylococcs aureus bacteria, commonly known as MRSA (methicillin resistant Staphylococcus aureus) which is normally harmless but is resistant to potent antibiotics, and can be fatal to someone who is already weak or ill, such as people in hospitals. Most infections can be treated with antibiotics such as methicillin, but overuse has helped create many bacteria that are resistant to antibiotics. This means it is more important than ever to improve immunity. Studies have found that certain compounds in British Blackcurrants are effective at inhibiting MRSA growth and can also stop reproduction of many other destructive bacteria including Salmonella and Listeria.[86]

3. Studies have shown concentrated blackcurrant may be an effective anti-depressant.

4. Eye strain, visual fatigue and blurry vision may be increasing due to the widespread use of computers and video display terminals (VDTs) at home and work. Carotenoids, long-chain polyunsaturated fatty acids, and anthocyanosides have been shown to enhance visual acuity. Intake of anthocyanoside-rich foods may help ease or prevent vision problems. In a recent study, a powdered concentrate of Black Currant was found to consist of four anthocyanoside components, similar to but simpler than bilberry. Oral intake of the black currant extract lowered the dark adaptation threshold in a double-blind, placebo-controlled, crossover study with human subjects. Black currant also counteracted the eye strain related to computer operation according to participants' subjective analysis.

Greens & Berries

What are the hottest new ways to get berry goodness? Combination supplements! Antioxidants work together and the development of new combination products allow consumers to get a blend of the health supporting nutrients from berries and other healthy foods.

New berry blends combine 36:1 concentrations of blueberry, cranberry, strawberry and raspberry, for an ORAC of 4000! By adding acai (ah-saw'-ee), pomegranate, pineapple, as well as mango and black currant, this powder can be mixed with water for a delicious, free radical-fighting beverage providing extra energy, brain nutrition, circulatory support and immune enhancement. Look for berry blends on their own or as an ingredient in food supplements.

Health Benefits

Concentrated berries mix well with antioxidant-rich green foods, such as spirulina, barley grass, wheat grass, alfalfa and chlorella. The latter are often called superfoods because of their high nutritional value. While these aren't berries, you will find them mixed with berry extracts in many new products. If you're serious about intensifying your antioxidant levels, this is another way to do so.

Greens can:
- help increase antioxidant protection
- improve cellular energy production
- reduce inflammation and pain
- enhance circulation

Greens and Berries may contain:

Spirulina, a rich source of carotenoids from the sea.
- up to 71% complete protein, (more than meat, fish or poultry)
- rich in B vitamins, minerals, enzymes
- includes essential fats
- powerful antioxidant phytochemicals

Chlorella, a marine algae
- high in protein
- contains B vitamins, minerals, carotenoids
- also vitamin E and chlorophyll
- shown to have antitumor and antiviral activity

Barley Grass and Wheat Grass
- rich in chlorophyll
- B vitamins
- protein
- minerals
- flavonoids
- enzymes
- more iron than spinach

Alfalfa — named the 'great healer' by herbalists
- Traditionally used to treat digestive disturbances and arthritis
- an excellent source of chlorophyll
- B vitamins
- vitamin K
- vitamin E,
- beta carotene
- amino acids
- plant enzymes

A combination of berry concentrates and potent green extracts can give you the equivalent of 5 to 9 servings of fruits and vegetables with incredible convenience. Some products are in a mixable powder, to be stirred into water or juice – a delicious way to feed fruits and vegetables to broccoli-hating kids and teens! Others berry/green combinations can be found in capsules for even greater convenience.

Research Summary

1. Research into the antioxidant capacity of blended greens has shown these to be an excellent source of concentrated nutrients. More and more combination products are being developed and additional research is being conducted. Results can be expected in the near future.

Berries for Life. A natural way to stay younger.

Berries
A natural way to stay younger, longer.

No one likes to lose their youthful energy and abilities. Preventing and slowing aging of the body is not just vanity, living a long and vibrant life is something most people desire. So, how can berries help?

With more and more scientific studies being conducted on foods and nutraceuticals, more ways are being found to slow the aging process and enhance health. Berries and their phytochemical components are high on the list of affordable, natural ways to stay "younger" longer.

From Top to Bottom

To summarize the health support berries can provide let's look at the body from the top down.

The Brain
Anthocyanosides and antioxidant support for the brain can prevent free radical damage and improve circulation for better brain function.

The Eyes
Age-related macular degeneration (AMD) affects one in three people over 75 years of age and can start much earlier. Usually painless, AMD can begin as blurry vision, darkness or distortion in the center of the visual field. Damage can occur to the eyes, including blindness, due to complications of diabetes. Glaucoma, caused by pressure within the eye, and cataracts, a cloudy formation reducing clarity of vision and colour perception, are both linked to oxidation within the eye. Berries with their powerful antioxidant action are key dietary allies in the prevention of vision loss.

The Heart
Heart disease, high cholesterol, high blood pressure all respond well to increased dietary antioxidants and the healthy fibre provided by most berries. Blueberries, cranberries, pomegranate, strawberries and cherries are among the leaders in heart health support, but be sure to also take advantage of nature's heart helpers, Omega-3 fatty acids, green tea, fruits, vegetables and whole grains.

The Lungs
Blackberry, raspberry and elderberry are helpful as expectorants (substances that clear phlegm and induce coughing to clear the lungs).

The Pancreas
Diabetes and its complications affect millions. Elevated blood glucose levels can cause a reaction between proteins that make up blood vessel walls and glucose; reactions that can damage blood vessels especially in the eyes, nerves, kidneys and heart. Managing glucose levels, with insulin or through diet and lifestyle modifications, is essential to avoid the life-shortening complications of diabetes. High antioxidant foods such as blueberries, high fibre and specialized phytochemicals such as anthocyanins and quercetin, have been shown to improve the health of blood vessels, improve immunity and help balance blood sugar.

The Digestive Tract
Cranberries specifically have been shown to help prevent or reduce the impact of peptic ulcers. Strawberries have long been used to ease diarrhea and dysentery. Blackberries and raspberries can ease intestinal inflammation.

The Urinary Tract
Again, cranberries and cranberry extract are nature's best known protection from UTIs, urinary tract infections, thanks to their anti-adherence properties. Blueberries and blueberry extract have some of the same activity. Berries high in tannins have diuretic action as well.

The Bowels
The natural fibre in berries helps promote regularity and some berries, specifically elderberry, have additional laxative properties.

The Circulatory System
Keeping blood circulating freely through the body is a basic health requirement and poor circulation contributes to many illnesses and conditions. Antioxidant berries, with blueberries being star performers, improve capillary strength and integrity, inhibit free radical damage and improve the tone of the cardiovascular system for better overall health. Some berries also reduce the stickiness of platelets. Berries with greens also enhance circulation.

The Joints
Inflammation and pain of arthritis can be alleviated with improved circulation. Cherries, cranberries and blueberries are especially valued for their circulatory enhancement and anti-inflammatory properties. They contain natural compounds that help control pain, inflammation and swelling.

The Legs and Feet
Although the herbs butcher's broom and horse chestnut are the most recommended for varicose veins and chronic venous insufficiency (poor circulation and leg cramping), these symptoms may also respond positively to increased antioxidant intake. Circulation, especially in the brain and extremities (hands and feet) improves with added dietary bioflavonoids and antioxidants.

Overall Health & Risk Reduction
According to the USA's National Cancer Institute, "people whose diets are rich in fruits and vegetables have a lower risk of getting cancers of the lung, mouth, pharynx (throat), esophagus, stomach, colon and rectum. They are also less likely to get cancers of the breast, pancreas, ovaries, larynx and bladder." Recommended intake is 5 to 9 servings per day of fruits and vegetables, and the more colourful they are, the better!

Ellagic acid and Quercetin are two plant compounds that are showing promise for their cancer-fighting properties. They may inhibit abnormal cell development. Raspberries and blackberries, cranberries and strawberries contain significant amounts of ellagic acid.

Immunity is enhanced by increased intake of antioxidant rich foods. Berries with their high vitamin C content and other antioxidant compounds support a strong immune system.

Preventing the most serious of illnesses, heart disease, cancer and diabetes for a start, is one of the most important reasons for increasing one's intake of the beneficial phytochemicals found in beautiful berries. If fresh berries are not available, their concentrated goodness can be added to the diet throughout the year by incorporating frozen berries, berry juices, berry supplements, extracts and concentrates.

Berries for Life. A natural way to stay younger.

68

The moral of the story.

Pick berries. Freeze them.
Eat them daily. Stay healthy.

When the freezer is empty, buy berry jams or juices (but watch out for too much sugar content) or "pick" some berries from the shelf of your nearest pharmacy in the form of berry concentrates and extracts. Look on the labels of berry supplements for standardized (guaranteed) high levels of active compounds and for potent concentrations. You can find 5 to 1 concentrates or even 36 to 1, which means that 36 grams of berries are concentrated into 1 gram of berry supplement!

This overview of the life-enhancing power of berries is not conclusive. New research is being done every month and more knowledge will allow us all to live longer, healthier, happier lives—as long as we use it to help ourselves and our families.

Enjoy!

Dr. Joyce Tellier Johnson

References

1. Oligomeric proanthocyanidins - OPCs – Monograph. Alternative Medicine Review.2003. Volume 8, Number 4; P: 442-450.

2. Cooper DA, Eldridge AL, Peters JC. Dietary carotenoids and certain cancers, heart disease, and age-related macular degeneration: a review of recent research. Nutr Rev. 1999; 57:201-14.

3. Stoner, G.D. Natural chemical in strawberries may decrease risk of cancer. USDA Agricultural Research Service.

4. Antioxidant Flavonoids: Structure, Function and Clinical Usage. Alternative Medicine Review, 1996; Volume 1, Number 2; P: 103-111.

5. Diane H. Morris, PhD, RD. flax - A Health and Nutrition Primer. Available: http://www.flaxcouncil.ca/english/index.php?p=primer&mp=nutrition [2006, November 18].

6. Quercetin-Monograph. Alternative Medicine Review. 2001; Volume 3, Number 2; P: 140-143.

7. Ingster LM, Feinleib M. Could salicylates in food have contributed to the decline in cardiovascular disease mortality? A new hypothesis. American Journal Of Public Health. 1997 Sep; Vol. 87 (9), pp. 1554-7.

8. Driscoll Strawberry Associates. Berry Health Benefits [Online]. Available: http://www.driscolls.com/health/benefits.html [2006, November 18].

9. Howell A.B., Vorsa N., Der Marderosian A., Foo L.Y. "Inhibition of the adherence of P-fimbriated Escherichia coli to uroepithelial-cell surfaces by proanthocyanidin extracts from cranberries." The New England Journal of Medicine. 1998. 339:15: 1085.

10. Bagchi D., Sen C., Bagchi M., and Atalay M. "Anti-angiogenic, antioxidant, and anti-carcinogenic properties of a novel anthocyanin-rich berry extract formula." Journal of Biochemistry (Moscow). 2004. 69:1:75-80.

11. Joseph, J.A., et al. 1999. Reversals of age-related declines in neuronal signal transduction, cognitive, and motor behavioral deficits with blueberry, spinach, or strawberry dietary supplementation. Journal of Neuroscience 1999(Sept. 15);19(18):8114-21.

12. Sweeney MI, Kalt W, MacKinnon SL, Ashby J, Gottschall-Pass KT. Feeding rats diets enriched in lowbush blueberries for six weeks decreases ischemia-induced brain damage. Nutr Neurosci. 2002 Dec; 5(6): 427-31.

13. Jean Mayer, USDA Human Nutrition Research Center on Aging found: Blueberries can reverse age-related declines in brain function, namely cognitive and motor deficits with Alzheimer's and Parkinson's disease.

14. Lau FC, Shukitt-Hale B, Joseph JA. The beneficial effects of fruit polyphenols on brain aging. Neurobiol Aging. 2005 Dec;26 Suppl 1:128-32. Epub 2005 Sep 27.

15. Prior, RL, et. al. J of Agric. Food Chem. 1998, 46:2686-2693 Bickford, P.C. et. al. Society for Neuroscience Abs. 1998, 24: 2157.

16. Heinenen, L.M. et al. J. Agric. Food Chem. 1998, 46:4107-4112 Howell, A.B. and V. Nicholi. New Engl. J. Med 1998, 339: 1085-1086.

17. Rimando AM, Kalt W, Magee JB, Dewey J, Ballington JR. Resveratrol, pterostilbene, and piceatannol in vaccinium berries. J Agric Food Chem. 2004 Jul 28; 52(15):4713-9.

18. Lila, M. "Anthocyanins and human health: an in vitro investigative approach." Journal of Biomedicine and Biotechnology. 2004. 5: 306-313.

19. Nair M., Kandaswami C. et al. Grape seed extract proanthocyanidins downregulate HIV- 1 entry coreceptors, CCR2b, CCR3 and CCR5 gene expression by normal peripheral blood mononuclear cells. Biol Res 35: 421-431, 2002.

20. Amy Howell. Research update on beneficial medicinal compounds in blueberries. Available: http://www.cook.rutgers.edu/~bluecran/medicinalgeneralinfopage.htm [2006, November 18].

21. Agnes M. Rimando, Rangaswamy Nagmani, et al. Pterostilbene, a New Agonist for the Peroxisome Proliferator-Activated Receptor -Isoform, Lowers Plasma Lipoproteins and Cholesterol in Hypercholesterolemic Hamsters. J. Agric. Food Chem.; 2005; 53(9) pp 3403 – 3407.

22. USDA. Agriculture Research Services. Pterostilbene's Healthy Potential-Berry compound may inhibit breast cancer and heart disease. Available: http://www.ars.usda.gov/is/AR/archive/nov06/health1106.htm [2006, November 18].

23. Jayle GE and Aubert L; Action des des glucosides d'anthocyanes sur la vision scotopique et mesopique du sujet normal. Therapie 19, 171-185, 1964.

24. Terrasse J and Moinade S : Premier resulatats obtenus avec un nouveau facteur vitaminique P « les anthocyanosides » extratis du Vaccinium myrtillus. Press Med 72, 397-700, 1964.

25. Andres-Lacueva C, Shukitt-Hale B, Galli RL, Jauregui O, Lamuela-Raventos RM, Joseph JA. Anthocyanins in aged blueberry-fed rats are found centrally and may enhance memory. Nutr Neurosci 2005;8(2):111-20.

26. Sweeney MI; Kalt W; MacKinnon SL; Ashby J; Gottschall-Pass KT. Feeding rats diets enriched in lowbush blueberries for six weeks decreases ischemia-induced brain damage. Nutritional Neuroscience, 2002 Dec; Vol. 5 (6), pp. 427-31.

27. Zheng W, Wang SY. "Oxygen radical absorbing capacity of phenolics in blueberries, cranberries, chokeberries, and lingoberries," Journal of Agricultural and Food Chemistry, 2003, 51:502-509

28. Kowalchuk J. Antiviral Activity of Fruit Extracts. J Food Science. 41: 1013-1017, 1976.

29. The Cranberry Institute. Health Research. Avalable: http://www.cranberryinstitute.org/healthresearch.htm. [2006, November 18]

30. Nakaishi H. Effects of black current anthocyanoside intake on dark adaptation and VDT work-induced transient refractive alteration in healthy humans. Alt Med Rev 2000 Dec; 5 (6):553-62.

31. Avorn J, Monane M, Gurwitz JH, Glynn RJ, Choodnovskiy I, Lipsitz LA. Reduction of bacteriuria and pyuria after ingestion of cranberry juice. Journal of the American Medical Association 1994; 271: 751-754.

32. Walker EB, Barney DP, Mickerlsen JN, Walton RJ, Mickelsen RAJr. Cranberry concentrate: UTI prophylaxis. The Journal of Family Practice 1997; 45: 167-168.

33. Kontiokari T, Sundqvist K, Nuutinen M, Pokka T, Koskela M, Uhari M. Randomised trial of cranberry-lingonberry juice and Lactobacillus GG drink for the prevention of urinary tract infections in women. British Medical Journal 2001; 322: 1571-1575.

34. Stothers L. A randomized trial to evaluate effectiveness and cost effectiveness of naturopathic cranberry products as prophylaxis against urinary tract infection in women. The Canadian Journal of Urology 2002; 9: 1558-1562.

35. Sobota AE. Inhibition of bacterial adherence by cranberry juice: potential use for the treatment of urinary tract infections. The Journal of Urology 1984; 131: 1013-1016.

36. Ofek I, Goldhar J, Zafriri D, Lis H, Adar R, Sharon N. Anti-Escherichia coli adhesion activity of cranberry and blueberry juices. New England Journal of Medicine 1991; 324: 1599.

37. Howell AB, Vorsa N, Marderosian AD, Foo LY. Inhibition of the adherence of p-fimbriated Escherichia coli to uroepithelial-cell surfaces by proanthocyanidin extracts from cranberries. The New England Journal of Medicine 1998; 339: 1085.

38. Howell AB, Leahy M, Kurowska E, Guthrie N. In vivo evidence that cranberry proanthocyanidins inhibit adherence of p-fimbriated *E. coli* bacteria to uroepithelial cells. Federation of American Societies for Experimental Biology Journal 2001; 15: A284.

39. Foxman B, Geiger AM, Palin K, Gillespie B, Koopman JS. First-time urinary tract infection and sexual behavior. Epidemiology 1995; 6: 162-168.

40. Dignam RR, Ahmed M, Kelly KG, Denman SJ, Zayon M, Kleban M.The effect of cranberry juice on urinary tract infection rates in a long-term care facility. Annals of Long-Term Care 1998; 6: 163-167.

41. Kontiokari T, Laitinen J, Jarvi L, Pokka T, Sundqvist K, Uhari M. Dietary factors protecting women from urinary tract infection. American Journal of Clinical Nutrition 2003; 77: 600-604.

42. Manges AR, Johnson JR, Foxman B, O'Bryan TT, Fullerton KE, Riley LW. Widespread distribution of urinary tract infections caused by a multidrug-resistant Escherichia coli clonal group. The New England Journal of Medicine 2001; 345: 1007-1013.

43. Stamm WE. An epidemic of urinary tract infections. The New England Journal of Medicine 2001; 345: 1055-1057.

44. Howell AB, Foxman B. Cranberry juice and adhesion of antibiotic-resistant uropathogens. Journal of the American Medical Association 2002; 287.

45. Henig YS, Leahy MM. Cranberry juice and urinary-tract health: Science supports folklore. Nutrition 2000; 16: 684-687.

46. FC, Fagelman E. Cranberry juice and urinary tract infections: what is the evidence? Urology 2001; 57: 407-413.

47. Leahy M, Roderick R, Brilliant K. The cranberry - promising health benefits, old and new. Nutrition Today 2001; 36: 254-265.

48. Howell AB, Reed J, Winterbottom R, Krueger C. Bacterial anti-adhesion activity of cranberry vs. other foods. Federation of American Societies for Experimental Biology 2002.

49. Ruel G . Changes in plasma antioxidant capacity and oxidized low-density lipoprotein levels in men after short-term cranberry juice consumption., Metabolism. 2005 Jul; 54(7):856-61.

50. Bomser, J., et al. In vitro anticancer activity of fruit extracts from Vaccinium species. Planta Medica, 1996. 62: 212-216.

51. Verma, A.K., et al. Inhibition of 7,12-dimethylbenz(a) anthracene- and N-nitrosemethylurea-induced rat mammary cancer by dietary flavonol quercitin. Cancer Res. 1988; 48(20):5754-5758.

52. Weiss EI, Lev-Dor R, Sharon N, Ofek I. Inhibitory Effect of high-molecular-weight constituent of cranberry on adhesion of oral bacteria. Critical Reviews in Food Science & Nutrition, 2002. 42(Suppl.): 285-292.

53. Krueger, C.G., Porter, M.L., Weibe, D.A., Cunningham, D.G., and Reed, J.D. Potential of cranberry flavonoids in the prevention of copper-induced LDL oxidation. Polyphenols Communications, 2000. Freising-Weihenstephan (Germany). 2: 447-448.

54. Reed, J. Cranberry flavonoids, atherosclerosis and cardiovascular health. Critical Reviews in Food Science & Nutrition, 2002. 42(Suppl.): 301-316.

55. Wilson, T., Porcari, J.P. and Harbin, D. Cranberry extract inhibits low density lipoprotein oxidation. Life Sciences, 1998. 62(24): 381-386.

56. Burger O, Weiss E, Sharon N, Tabak M, Neeman I, and Ofek I. Inhibition of Helicobacter pylori adhesion to human gastric mucus by a high-molecular-weight constituent of cranberry juice. Critical Reviews in Food Science & Nutrition, 2002. 42(Suppl.).

57. James F.Balch, M.D. & Phyllis A. Balch, C.N.C., Prescription for Nutritional Healing, (Avery Publishing,1997).

58. Jellin JM, Gregory P. batz F, Hitchens K, burson S, Shaver K, Palacioz K, editos. Natural Medicines Comprehensive database. Stockton (CA): Therapeutic Research Faculty; 2006.

59. Pantuck, A.J., et al., Phase II Study of Pomegranate Juice for Men with Rising Prostate-Specific Antigen following Surgery or Radiation for Prostate Cancer., Clin Cancer Res. 2006 Jul 1;12(13):4018-4026.

60. Kaplan M, Hayek T, Raz A, Coleman, Dornfeld L, Vaya J, Aviram M. Pomegranate juice supplementation to atherosclerotic mice reduces macrophage lipid peroxidation, cellular cholesterol accumulation and development of atherosclerosis. Biochemical and Molecular Action of Nutrients 2001 Aug;131(8):2082-9.

61. Aviram M, Dornfeld L, Kaplan M, et al. Pomegranate juice flavonoids inhibit low-density lipoprotein oxidation and cardiovascular diseases: studies in atherosclerotic mice and humans. Drugs under experimental and clinical Research Vol XXVIII, NO 2/3 49-62 (2002).

62. Fuhrman B, Volkova N, Aviram M. Pomegranate juice inhibits oxidized LDL uptake and cholesterol biosynthesis in macrophages. J Nutr Biochem. 2005 Sep;16(9):570-6.

63. Sumner MD, Elliott-Eller M, Weidner G, Daubenmier JJ, Chew MH, Marlin R, Raisin CJ, Ornish D. Effects of pomegranate juice consumption on myocardial perfusion in patients with coronary heart disease. Am J Cardiol. 2005 Sep 15; 96(6):810-4.

64. Huang TH, Peng G, Kota BP, Li GQ, Yamahara J, Roufogalis BD, Li Y. Anti-diabetic action of Punica granatum flower extract: activation of PPAR-gamma and identification of an active component. Toxicol Appl Pharmacol. 2005 Sep 1;207(2):160-9.

65. Aviram M, et al. Pomegranate juice consumption for 3 years by patients with carotid artery stenosis reduces common carotid intima-media thickness, blood pressure and LDL oxidation. Clin Nutr. 2004 Jun;23(3):423-33.

66. Sastravaha G, Gassmann G, Sangtherapitikul P, Grimm WD. Adjunctive periodontal treatment with Centella asiatica and Punica granatum extracts in supportive periodontal therapy. J Int Acad Periodontol. 2005 Jul; 7(3):70-9.

67. Aviram, M. Atherosclerosis, Aug. 2006; vol 187: pp 363-371.

68. Rosenblat M, Hayek T, Aviram M. Anti-oxidative effects of pomegranate juice (PJ) consumption by diabetic patients on serum and on macrophages. Atherosclerosis. 2005 Oct 11 [Epub ahead of print].

69. Ahmed, S., Wang, N., Hafeez, B.B., Cheruvu, V.K., and Haqqi, T.M. Punica granatum L. extract inhibits IL-1ß–induced expression of matrix metalloproteinases by inhibiting the activation of MAP kinases and NF-k in human chondrocytes in vitro. J. Nutr. 2005; 135: 2096-2102.

70. Chang, R.I. et al. Effect of ellagic acid and hydroxylated flavonoids on the tumorigenicity of benzo(a)pyrene and ±7b, 8a-dihydroxy-9a, 10a-epoxy-7,8,9,10-tetrahydrobenzo(a)pyrene on mouse skin and in the newborn mouse. Carcinogenesis 1985. 6:1127-1133.

71. Labrecque, L. et al. Combined inhibition of PDGF and VEGF receptors by ellagic acid, a dietary-derived phenolic compound. Carcinogenesis. 2005. April; 26(4):821-6. Italics ours..

72. Falsaperla M. et al. Support ellagic acid therapy in patients with hormone refractory prostate cancer (HRPC) on standard chemotherapy using vinorelbine and estramustine phosphate. Eur Urol. 2005. Apr; 47(4):449-54.

73. Sterling, Marilyn. Got Anthocyanins? Nutrition Science News December 2001.

74. Kamei, H. et al. Suppression of tumor cell growth by anthocyanins in vitro. Cancer Invest. 1995. 13: 590-594.

75. Mertens-Talcott, SU et al. Ellagic acid potentiates the effect of quercetin on p21 waf1/cip1, p53, and MAP-kinases without affecting intracellular generation of reactive oxygen species in vitro. J. Nutr. 2005 Mar; 135 (3): 609-614.

76. Kresty LA, Morse MA, Morgan C, Carlton PS, Lu J, Gupta A, Blackwood M, Stoner GD. Chemoprevention of esophageal tumorigenesis by dietary administration of lyophilized black raspberries. Cancer Res 2001;61:6112-6119.

77. The Ohio State University. University Medical Center- School of Allied Medical Professions; Black Raspberries: 'Fruitraceuticals' of the Future. Available: http://amp.osu.edu/md/article.cfm?id=2602 [2006, November 18].

78. The Ohio State University. Research News- Black Raspberries show multiple defenses in thwarting cancer. Available: http://www.oregon-berries.com/cx15/blackraspshow.pdf [2006, November 18].

79. Min Ding, Rentian Feng, et. al., Cyanidin-3-glucoside, a Natural Product Derived from Blackberry, Exhibits Chemopreventive and Chemotherapeutic Activity, J. Biol. Chem., Vol. 281, Issue 25, 17359-17368, June 23, 2006.

80. Matchett MD, Mackinnon SL, Sweeney MI, Gottschall-Pass KT, Hurta RA. Blueberry flavonoids inhibit matrix metalloproteinase activity in DU145 human prostate cancer cells. Biochem Cell Biol. 2005 Oct; 83(5): 637-43.

81. Maher P, Akaishi T, Abe K. Flavonoid fisetin promotes ERK-dependent long-term potentiation and enhances memory. Proc Natl Acad Sci U S A. 2006 Oct 31; 103(44):16568-73. Epub 2006 Oct 18.

82. Burkhardt et al., (2002). Detection and Quantification of the Antioxidant Melatonin in Montmorency and Balaton Tart Cherries (Prunus cerasus) J. Agric. Food Chem. 49(10): 4898-4902.

83. Julie Beattie, Alan Crozier and Garry G. Duthie, Potential Health Benefits of Berries. Current Nutrition & Food Science, 2005, 1, 71-86.

84. Sambucus nigra (Elderberry) - Monograph. Alternative Medicine Review. 2005, Volume 10, Number 1 P: 51-55.

85. Zichria Zachay-Rones, Ph.D., Noemi Varsano, M.Sc., et. al., Inhibition of Several Strains of Influenza Virus in Vitro and Reduction of Symptoms by an Elderberry Extract (Sambucus Nigra L.) During an Outbreak of Influenza B Panama, Journal of Alternative and Complementary Medicine, 1995: 1, 361-369.

86. H Cavanagh ,Antibacterial Activity of Berry Fruits Used for Culinary Purposes. Journal of Medicinal Food. 2003.Vol. 6, No. 1: 57-61.

87. Effects of Black Currant Anthocyanoside Intake on Dark Adaptation and VDT Work-induced Transient Refractive Alteration in Healthy Humans, Altern Med Rev 2000; 5(6): 553-562.

88. Jie Sun, Yi-Fang Chu, Xianzhong Wu, and Rui Hai Liu. Antioxidant and Antiproliferative Activities of Common Fruits. J. Agric. Food Chem., 50 (25), 7449 -7454, 2002.